men

fall   **7**

baby   9

vignettes on encounters with three men   10

this week   12

repeat   13

writing poems in English class   14

not mountainside nor city block   15

landscape   16

quantifying and qualifying my days   17

bookends   18

x is for   19

power   21

trimmed branches   22

intersecting   24

euphoric   25

winter   **27**

forgot   29

drop   30

change   32

win   33

omens   34

sight   35

space   36

winter walls   38

apartment 108   40

met   41

brooms   43

choices   44

red   45

here   46

beaches   48

spring   **49**

belt   51

yet   53

inherit   54

bloody   55

burning   57

both   58

homes   59

awakening   60

pastels   62

smyth   63

always been   65

footprints   66

topsail   67

forever stares back   68

between lakes   69

buried   70

tornado alley   71

night vision   72

summer   **73**

flow   75

watson   77

summer   78

war	79
unapologetic	80
whole foods basket	82
youth	84
lists	85
confusing lovers with lovers	87
hail	88
net	89
temple	90
eyes	91
seeds	93
hands	94
vowels	95
reach	96
men	97
about the author	**99**

fall

baby

at fourteen she told me
she'd lost her virginity
in the hot tub
do it in water
she said
it's easier than the bed
in the guest room
of a friend's friend's parents' house
a creaky antique bed
an unathletic bed
that broke the second time
wooden splinters scattered
among laughter
hushed and jagged
writing about love is easy
low hanging stone fruit
writing about men
and women
who love men
and women
luscious and jagged
like me
like the mountain
like the knife against my throbbing neck
like indie bookstore poetry reads
like babies with teeth
a baby at fourteen

vignettes on encounters with three men

I don't remember
the first time we met
but you claim it happened
and now you tell me
that you remember me
because I make people
fall in love with me
you tell me
I have that power
I laugh
and smile
your face changes
and you say
take it easy on them

our shoulders brush
and burn
with first day of school butterflies
buzzing between
our adjacent bodies
when I look at you
I make you look at me
I tell you
I am good
at getting the people I want
you give me a look
that says
take it easy on me

your speed dial is 4

I tell you
I have something to tell you
I murmur about maybe mistakes
too many dark rooms
and drunk nights
I hear you nod your head
politely
supportively
but really
what you want to say is
take it easy

this week

This is a poem about burls on trees
A gold necklace shaped like a ginkgo leaf
One I kept instead of making her keep
Rooted with Artemis down in the deep
Trees know each November they have to sleep
They know each green spring returns us the
    bees
They know winter beaches have whiter seas
They know when spirit worlds are within reach
They know their leaves keep our breathing air
    clean
They know rings grow whether soften or
    seethe
They know when it's time to spread and sow
    seeds
They know how to whisper just what they need
They know their buds arrive early indeed
As the changing earth continues to heat
The breaking point was a shattering sweep
Now I'm drinking tea while tied on my knees
New dendritic pink ink has got me weak
Reclaiming names isn't meant to be mean
Under covers alone I'm still not free
Pentameter flows yet can't leave it be
Sometimes it's hard to go slow at this speed
I can break the glass in emergencies
This is a poem about burls on trees

repeat

when you're not here you're hard to find
perhaps you've been carried off by the wind   13
I'm in the spaces between your fingers and
  teeth
constant like your can't-stop breath

writing poems in English class

I never listen to lecture;
the melodic monotony, a catalyst for creativity.
Instead of analyzing anapests,
pen to page I write--
poems, mostly.
I steal a glance at the scrawled stanza
sitting on the desk of the boy two seats over;
his poetic musings
on parting ways with a lover.
Apparently no one takes notes
in English class.

not mountainside nor city block

I went into the woods to forget you
but the dappled light on the dead leaves was
   the color of your skin
the tangled roots the color of your trying eyes
the shuddering wind the warmth of your
   whispering breath
there is nowhere I could go that isn't you

landscape

On that stony desert precipice,
I remember sitting sunset,
empty of my mother,
watched over by your mother.
Squinting at cool blues, blood reds,
you and I so softly kiss.

I wore my camera like sunglasses.
You told me, *let it go.*
I snapped up sunspots
and thought about home,
calmed by the wind
through the desert grasses.

Though unwelcome the sounds,
true fears scream through dreams.
Dreams I should transcribe at dawn,
but when I awaken,
sometimes quite shaken,
my pen seems to weigh a thousand pounds.

There I sat clicking pictures,
eyes stretched over the plain.
We were two desert fixtures
like the prickly cacti.
We pricked our twenty fingers,
releasing our blood red pain.

quantifying and qualifying my days

I spelled out "fax it"
and "nerdz"
with the magnets
on your refrigerator.

I sat on the couch
that you got for free
off Craig's list.

I made salad
with avocados
while you cooked pasta
from an open box
that we found
in the pantry.

I leaned over you
at the counter
and stopped you
from cutting the tomatoes
because you were doing it
wrong.

bookends

burnt out bedrooms
lake of green
stars dead too
inn railing lean

stolen black cat
spinning on sleet
gametime cut slack
thanksgiving meal eat

blue quilted bed
lighting the high
wrists behind head
an inspiring sunrise

the library meet
two briefcases black
preparing a feast
hunger is back

eyes of lake
the official begin
highway at daybreak
gray home again

x is for

xenophobic zeitgeist
think twice
make nice
call home
xylophone
ding dong ditch
in the pitch
black
in the dark
with the sharks
ring-a-ding
loaded spring
cringing and bristling
bustling and hustling
cluttered with shattered glass
a scattered mass
that clattered down
like little bits of matter
of the kids in class
they pull your hair
tear your knees
distal seas
proximal proclivity
pro clavicle
miraculous
downright acrobatical
it's maniacal
sub riotal
pivotal
post periodical
hypnotic
doctorate

don't count on it
or to three
snap
stay with me
stingrays and tapestries
wind for kites
wings for flight
suffice it to sacrifice
mitigate and minimize
daisy skies
like dizzy eyes
reeling but ready to rise
with etiquette
good rhetoric
hope it's copasetic
pathetic heretic
headlong running
blazing
humming
to baby carriages
boston marriages
mayday maelstroms
a bildungsroman
a building block for lives to live on
through 'til dawn
a subplot gone wrong
like frankensteen
no, frankenstein
well frankly, dear, this all sounds fine

power

I never wanted mindreading
As a superpower
Always teleportation
Shapeshifting second
But now
What I would give
To read the deep
To breathe underwater
In ocean caves
From each hemisphere
Analytical and intuitive
Icebergs and warm seas
Where I could travel in a blink
Become a fish
Or a sea urchin
Slip on slippery skin
Or thin black spines
Then blink back
Into mind's eye

trimmed branches

Foraging for puffballs in the forest
An amateur's take on the new normal
Mistakenly making lovelust formal
Tripping on syllables down the wormhole

Time to produce like a tree bearing fruit
Dripping wet words from inside the Earth's
  womb
Womanhood swept up with a trimmed-branch
  broom
Persimmons above, below deepest roots

Whispering to the goddess of kismet
Swimming angelfish seek to revisit
Black patterned stems growing up from
  fishnets
Planted three stars in sky cataclysmic.

Hide Orion's eyes from the lightning flash
Split desiccated earth in one fell blast
Cook turnips in cookbooks for succotash
The last meal the skies will ever rehash

Mothers move mountains from here to
  nowhere
Parrots for pirates flying through the air
Under lock and key remains the beachwear
One thousand reasons to start an affair

Thundering hooves from clipped-hair horses
Water the last of earthly resources
Would rather be lone but sleep in forces

Red barn the scene of cosmic divorces

Keep punching pillows, go on seeing red
Love, Cleopatra, and god are all dead
Persimmons and turnips allow well fed
Athena to battle, Mars was misled

Nature and divination twinned are here
Prescience palmistry keeps meeting deer
Recite sonnet one-thirty by Shakespeare
Muddy waters of aliveness unclear

Coral is coral, the sun is the sun
Snow roses need not outshine anyone
Seeing each being for beauty homespun
Comparison makes the Earth come undone

intersecting

Your silence the silent killer
Sticky snippets like post-its on pillars
The parallel lines of our tall towers
Toppled like mowed-over flowers
In the wake of our earthquake
The parallel lives we lived came awake
No way to avoid heartache
Not incense nor tarot
Nor skull of the sparrow
Nor crossbow and arrow
Nor eye of the pharaoh
Nor beaches too narrow
Will ever drag harrow
Through my bones and marrow
The way that our parallel lies
Made me see through your eyes
Down your throat to your chest
The cage where hearts rest
Beating bleeding blood into blue veins
I can see through your tan skin
Just like you can see through my clothes
All the way through down to my bones
Up to my eyes back down to my neck
Your neck a gateway drug
Scream myself awake from sleep's fog
Dream myself awake from alarms
It's those dreams that linger
Shocking like chopping and slicing a finger
Adrenaline-charged reaction time
Fingers in action ten parallel lines

euphoric

Driving down streets lined with wartime prices
Watching Euphoria while people are dying
Write lines about addicts lapsed
And bunker basement babies
Human cost of wartime tax
Doing lines like sniffing daisies
News off or on, still can't relax
Sitting slack jawed in class
Doing a hack job in math
Heavy lidded eyes of glass
Glazed behind shades of black
All hope lost that you will pass
Go home, no point in going back
Not about where you go
Not about what you know
But what you do and how you show
Love
Precious baby
Born into a world so crazy
Born to be the ones who save the
Earth
To save future mothers giving birth
To be the ones to trust your worth
Both babies, children of god
Both good and bad, both right and wrong
Vulnerable, strong
Crying through crises
Left unto their own devices
Deserted by mother earth
We abandoned her first
Every generation has the same dream
That the next generation is greater than we

winter

forgot

A world inhabited by secret habits,
In the year of the snake, you're not my rabbit.
You take what I make and say you're glad it
Fills me, how silly though
To spend time writing rhymes,
Sketching the lines I see in my mind,
While I drip down the drain in the meantime.
It's not just you--
Winter is just hard to get through.
After she died your light went out too.
Tried reigniting it but scorched my eyelashes,
So instead I battened down the hatches,
Bolted myself in the bathroom.
It didn't even have pennies on the floor,
The white tile wasn't shiny anymore,
Like the scraped-off brass on the bathroom
    door
Handle with the push-button lock.
Terrified to hear the knock,
But never did. You always forgot
I was in there.

drop

writing on coasters from bars
envelopes from the discard
bin, been saving my musings
my feelings confusing
I face forked-road ultimatums
pen love letters to well-known strangers
let lyrics sink in like they're part of my skin
knowing their poetry is written
for me alone, sitting at home
our skeletons are all made of bone
divide myself into quarters
one soul with four borders
what am I proving
with these mountains I'm moving?
by efforts strategical
my body is my soul's vehicle
I'm only a vessel
aren't we all special?
sewing holes and knowing souls
harder when I'm still not whole
can't show restraint while I'm restrained
without you it's not the same
in need of deep pressure
in need of deep pleasure
in need of streets with warmer weather
in need of my own aggressor
in need of whichever endeavor makes me light
    as a feather
clear as a bell
ringing loudly in hell
pull me up from the well

picking up paces
leaving bruised traces
softening in long embraces
if homeostasis is the goal
is it out of my control?
like the growing ozone hole
like all of the used-up coal
like being shot on grassy knoll
like sketchbooks of dusty charcoal
like holding hands atop consoles
like snowballs on a downward roll
like sipping from the sacred bowl
like ancestors on totem poles
from stolen lands of Seminoles

my white flag raised on this flagpole
dropping really takes its toll

change

signing the papers broke something loose
spare change came out like a wiggly tooth
bit an apple, pulled it out at the root

calling me baby, brunette, and sway
two paces, light speed or sit still and stay
inhabiting all on Christmas day

first time I've seen Orion in ten years
there was too much gas in the atmosphere
shattered glass doesn't matter, it's still crystal
  clear

brunette wavy head upon my chest
just one more snail story before rest
not good enough and I'm doing my best

this stage of anger is blaringly loud
regularly wrong yet both too proud
tried to take blame but I wasn't allowed

wishing for solar ovens under trees
the stove groans at our kitchen reprieve
knots shiny nylon rid us of dis-ease

wrapping her gifts didn't feel strange
under overpass, all our lives rearranged
pennies surely must be the smallest change

win

under candlecolored moon
brackish breakers exhumed
from sandy sepulchers
splash against the shore
while beachcombers touch cigarettes
to butane flames
bobsledders far away
would rather incinerate
than sit for one day longer
in birdless winter
daydreams of dogmushing
dismantled by the cold
I took a gaslamp
into the firestorm of your heart
to look around
we treated our bodies
like narcotics receptacles
you put me on a pedestal
like a state fair stuffed animal
there will always be
an isthmus between us
but I don't want to live
in the leanto of our future

omens

looking out in the dim
at augury ravens
omens of old patterns
found four mystic seasons
the red delivery
of monthly moon phases
twelve white lunar cycles
jealous green luna moths
beaks of blackbirds on a
desultory worm search
slippy slimy squirmy
grin and bear it or grit
your teeth so smooth and white
tires in twinkle lights
roll home in the darkness
floors of smeared purple jam
bowl of copper pennies
lincoln memorials
orange kitchen scissors
one clear cracked water glass
crows gaze through gray windows
squawking for stale breadcrumbs
feathers shine blue black green
salt in their eyelashes
where beaks can't reach to preen
house filled with suns eyes wings
abundance of tokens
luck love death intertwined
wound tightly in your hair
burned brightly in my mind

sight

I asked for visions whole and flittering;
Imagery, shivers at delivery.
Eyes filled with tears when you said you
    dreamed it.
I try to whisper but sometimes scream it.

Elegant creature, ferocious creature,
You drank of her deeply into your throat,
Where lingering fingers hover and float,
Unsure if they will ever quite reach her.

space

blue ridge brown mountain
fog hanging in the valley
branches a lime green galaxy
lichen-coated like night's black rhapsody
we hiked the hard acorn acre
relying on the ice and glass breaker
confessing sins to the religion forsaker
trusting intuition of the earthshaker
last will a mushroom undertaker
just another of god's green partakers
hanging in the door of the peacemaker
like a gravity feed on a sideways tree
rooted strong at ninety degrees
grouped along edges of experimental forests
dampened by fresh rain before us
deafened by mystery mechanical chorus
coated and covered in mountain laurel
an altar of options immoral
laid bare by a yellow bird
lie of normalcy
stability
happiness
finding it
impossible
illogical
no space for second and third acts
instead staring at the same peeling birdbath
replaying the same black glitch cat
looped in the same repeating path
is that happiness?
is that consciousness?

is that holiness?
pray the rosary
pride of ownership
push the lawnmower
I became a pillar
fell off a high shelf
tall column became myself
I'm just a seeker asking to see
the lines skies gods tell me
I'm always free

winter walls

I'm terrified to hydroplane
in spinning out relationships
instead I'll sip champagne in rain
lest I meet the last eclipse

a mug of tea in palms warmed up
hot hazy steam like last night's kiss
if we don't drink from the same cup
it would be a painful miss

raging gray like hurricanes
the scalding tea spills down my chest
it stings and burns with searing pain
so good I can forget the rest

I'm contemplating boundaries
inherited or built by bricks
remind myself of war stories
hopeful that those morals stick

we spy on neighbors through the sleet
boots loudly crunching as we go
yet in your house my silent feet
tread on invisible tiptoe

let's raise a glass of bubbles to
surviving on these coldest days
whiskey spiked tea and ink of blue
spill out a debt I can't repay

winter hurts — how could I forget?
my brain and belly filled with fear

it all feels so familiar yet
there are a lot of firsts this year

apartment 108

torturous disorder
disheveled hair and thoughts
nailbeds bleed
antibodies border
scabbed edges of blood clots
seeking help I heed
the apothecary
burning god's book
making salve from the ashes
rubbing my wary
eyes I look
batting lids long lashes
covered in charred
Deuteronomy
bent laughing hard
at its theology
it's easy to laugh
when you're already dying
tombstone split in half
reads: *god was lying*
as I breath my last breath
and surrender to death
I hear myself saying
some might call it praying
if only my body were attuned
if only my system were immune

met

Speeding down a winding gravel road through
  foreign thorny winter woods
The horns on the hood of the man in the moon
  and my dim bumping headlights the only
  slivers of luminescence
Banging into eroding embankments in a rush to
  arrive
Missing someone I've only met once
Drive right into the open expensive well-lit foyer
Pull up to a custom-crafted butcher-block
  banquet table covered in charcuterie,
  surrounded by sleek people sipping
My tires under modern industrial chandeliers
  bolted to sweepingly high cedar-beamed
  ceilings
A spray of gravel spilling over onto polished
  concrete floor
Guests unconcerned
Someone else will clean that up
Masking myself calm as I search for you,
  unrecognizable to me by appearance
Wearing black, hair cut, mature
But my soul knows yours
My skin knows yours
The ice between my teeth
My hands on my own dress
Black, disheveled from dashing to this
  gathering, short like my hair, edged in lace
I can't remember when you touch me
Eyes relax and broaden to black
Your rumpled shirt over my dress, collar still
  stiff

Her in her long white bathrobe
Eyes black and relaxed, calm, an open
    doorway
Not invitation nor warning, just open
My peace fingers looped through the backs of
    black shoes
Ready to wake up and walk home barefoot to
    you

brooms

I almost broke my left hand this morning,
pinned and crushed between the dragon and
the dumpster. I could ice it inside, or I could sit
under the pale sky and submerge it in snow
that's buried my tires. I'm so tired. I've stopped
to rest my hopes on you. With bruised hand
and muddy boots I'm leaving footprints in the
dust that fell out of the nicks in your body.

choices

fidgeting tongue flicking concentration
writing it down a new old sensation
tapping my way into next dimensions
breathing dreams of constricted suspension
women bleed each moon but still we survive
our wisdom to know it's not time to die
once in a blue moon there's no one to call
I'm a stand alone pillar after all
life is a new art form every day
sculpted from clay or marble chipped away
fresh linoleum carved out and printed
stamped like Lincoln on new pennies minted
is today bright copper or smeared graphite?
the choice is mine to be darkness or light

red

red
white red
hot bite red
won the fight red
lost in my head red
dried blood on the bed red
skin-tearing teeth-baring red
lipsticked-lips corset-wearing red
salvation and deliverance red
animalistic carnivorous red
meat tenderizer post-pulverize red
tantalizing appetizer red
new life grown from death graphic red
short black skirt stop traffic red
twilight sky pre-storm red
phoenix reborn red
grit your teeth red
stained sheets red
streets red
red

here

dealing with duality
plurality
multifaceted morality
chaste instructor
ardent lover
necessary mother
self-centered artist
sometimes smartest
born from stardust
hedonist
subservient
extroverted introvert
challenger
burned and been burned
a penny saved is a penny
for your thoughts
tied in knots
self-portraiture and apricots
leadership speaks louder
than a picture worth a thousand words
kill two birds
in the hand
in the bush
with one stone
stand on your own
cyclones and tombstones
writing from the storm cellar
essay edited — it's stellar
made some suggestions to tie it together
helpful
harmful
honest

drink deeply
from the straw that broke the camel's back
have a knack
for signs zodiac
cross that burned bridge
when you come to your senses
upended
upheaval
abhorrent
firestorms
tax breaks and insect swarms
discovery of new life forms
saltwater solution
new year's resolution
a one woman revolution

beaches

I dream of perfect and slant rhymes
make the excuse of scant time
would rather beat my body and trap my mind
than risk turning to what might unfold

words slip through the sieve into triplets
mind grieves as it goes on to give this
bruised up and used up old rhythmic
refrain about doing what I'm told

at the beach you would have been spiraling
contemplating untimely firings
but I answer to a higher thing than your anxiety
which is why I only went when it was cold

next year next year always next year or later
no kitchen conversation not sure which sin's
    greater
now I can sit in the sand in late days as fate
    were
came here because your shit was getting old

you tried to shoot me in my weakest spot
shot through with anger seething hot
but break my backbone you will not
your decision's got me feeling rather bold

I'm finally taking the time to write at night
praying my words still sound right in sunlight
because in the beach of my mind the sky is
    bright
as I wait for white waves to take hold

spring

belt

moon energy
celestial and silvery
glinting
glimmering
shimmery
minted
new moon-
faced coins
round and proud
freckling
the galaxy
reflecting
shallow seas
coins in the sky
stars in your eyes
cicadas rise
from perennial earth
one buzzing piece
of the universe
glistening
as you sit
on the curb
algal eyes
under sunglasses
dark as spread ashes
treating trees
like totems
playing telephone
since black October
woven
into the forest

into the final
the primal
the primitive
inquisitive
blistering
speckling
skin with freckles
unnoticed
with clothing
another insect
ethereal and evergreen
whispering

yet

This night is special
Realize Spring is in me forever
A sliver of silver tinsel
Moon's receding grace feels sinful
Mind racing with verbal need
Hand writing at mortal speed
Sunlight whispering to early buds
Almost but not yet, little one
Orion gets farther away every night
I'm waiting, I'm waiting, I'm biding my time
Spring, she is coming, yet not yet arrived
Spring, she is coming, again I've survived
Spring, she is coming, thank god I'm alive

inherit

I pray protections over you like fine mesh
They catch the light like spiderwebs
Spun in shimmery golden thread
I lay you down and kiss your head
I pray you abandon my recklessness
May your bullhead horns have a lighter weft
No crown of anger upon your head
As you grow may you inherit the rest
Active mind and fingers deft
To complement what you possess
As I lay you down to bed
I pray clear dreams hold you instead
Our hour together will come to an end
Not today but around the bend
I'll carry you with me 'til my last breath
In day and night, in life and death
Search your soul for deepest depths
Love each day for being fresh
Be yourself – no more, no less

bloody

functioning on autopilot
tried as I might
couldn't keep my light lit
so I turned it out
I went to sleep and stayed there
remaining awake too painful to bear
blisters on the roof of my mouth
from playing with fire
hollow in my heart no higher
power would allow us
to keep falling in love
with the earth and above
with each other
to be mothers
to be brothers
in arms, of the blade
when harm comes our way
I stayed numb for three thousand days
I succumbed to the brutal mundane
let the news fade away
let the scene fade to gray
'til the hue of a new day
glowed me awake
but why?
for bullets in the sky?
for our silent battle cry?
for children who can't stay alive?
we survived
you and I
if you're reading this you didn't die
but why?
to bring empty hands to gunfights?

to lie awake in fear at night?
to know dead kids can't see the sun shine
    bright?
god won't make it right
what I know how to do is write
I put it down in black and white
bloody words our world's birthright
born from bullet parasites
how will you pick up the fight?
love and hold your children tight
try hard to keep the good in sight
we have to be our own damn light

burning

tiptoeing through glass heat-shattered
remnants of the old house scattered
you quote my poems back to me
words about shells from bullets and the sea
once it's all written, what's left to write?
blowing candles out at night
flame-licked houses burning down
seeds in planters and pebbles on the ground
a fenced-in yard for my fenced-in heart
a fence to keep us arm's distance apart
how could any home measure up?
how could any house be enough?
how could anyone need just one?
we kneel before the temple tree
backyard blossoms tender pink
we pray to it for honesty
to say what we mean and what we need
a home in which we can be free
where alongside art we can be seen
a house built of love evergreen
these stairways and side doors of mine I'm still
    learning
locking the doors won't stop the house burning

both

For both Moon and Sun, it's torture that they
Must sleep 'cross the globe while the other's
  awake
Stars off in the distance burn out and fade
But Moon asks Sun to keep lighting the way
As they're left to imagine the other's heartache
Moon reflects truth while Sun warms the day
Both tasks important if Earth is to stay

homes

Awakened at five by my mind racing
We went back to the place of prayerful pacing
Spinning statues, infatuation
Driving through deforestation
Why are affirmations hard to come by?
Walking past spots where I used to hide
I'm drawn to people starting over
Well-established leads to boredom
Tracing my steps over curbs, along walls
Never felt safe enough before to let myself fall
I'm leaving this town in the rearview mirror
All I am is here

awakening

I left the room with the girl on the swing,
Found out I was leaving early last spring.
I simplify my words, stretch them out, make
  them sing,
But fuck all 'cause they never quite have that
  ring.

I'm stretched out in photographs on the ash
  floor.
On that cross-country trip I fell on a glass
  sword.
I ride with my feet propped up on your
  dashboard.
After this winter we're a bit short on cash for

A pair of new shoes to walk away from the
  news,
To race away from this winter's white blues,
Not much of a race if it's always lose-lose.
I'll run with you anywhere you choose.

Poetic lover, dark eyes, whitest witch,
From one to another I seamlessly switch.
In the final death you should scratch the itch,
It whispers to you in imperfect pitch.

Your first beer was fate, wished into existence.
We drained bottles and bowls in continued
  persistence.
Each line I write an act of resistance,
Halting anything done at other's insistence.

Looking backward at that black abyss,
I light a candle inside and reminisce,
Will we go our whole lives in ignorant bliss
without knowing what it feels like to kiss?

Awesome wind tugged my hair by little roots
It spoke to me in extreme absolutes.
It fed me figs and red passionfruit.
It stood me upright on feet resolute.

Those feet walked me out into the sea
To discover whether I'd sink or breathe.
I'm learning to listen to that voice in me,
Trusting intuition will set us free.

pastels

Soft hazy conversations
Whispered watercolor words
About lichen lifted up by birds
Peppered by blunt laughter
Shot through loud and bold
Sprinkled with meeting lips
Soundly sleep with no blindfold
Sweet lazing loving
Painting future sunsets
You kept me after green and gold
Finding healthy outlets
Continuing to make the choice
Your eyes see to my inky voice
Frida with her cigarettes
Choosing to stoop for change
To stretch to grow to wax to wane
Not painless but without regrets

smyth

on the bench that wrapped
around the concrete pillar
we spoke of Orion's killer
your strong arms wrapped
around monolith me
my heart still wrapped
for its remodeling
we told myths — we're wordsmiths
and jacks of all trade
battling inward an outward outrage
I will continue to flirt with
the grave
no coffin, no tomb
just sweet decay
goodbye to the man in night's womb
 — I'm okay —
that face in the moon
has so much to say
hidden behind black clouds over bleachers
none of us broken
just god's evolved creatures
interstellar clouds awoken
by three nebulas' collapsing features
my god pinned Orion in the sky
after the arrow caused his demise
he got pinned in the sky
he got placed way up high
he watches us all with his stardust eyes
when I die
let my body return
to feed mushrooms and insects
to grow into green fern

let my soul stay alive
to stargaze in the next life
to love hard
soul starred
(but still scarred) in the next life
now we wear our scars
as badges of knowing
that honesty is going
to be the only promise
worthy of bestowing
I promise
that change is the only constant
I'm showing you all of myself
I'm still growing

always been

past poems
picked over
split apart
and licked clean

the bones
of past lovers
used as picks
in our teeth

showed them
our knowing
but our words
ever mean

shifting homes
as we grow
cause we were
never seen

take it slow
let it flow
from the start
always been

footprints

gathering shells shaped like ears
bits like guitar picks
amassed in broad horizontal bands
along the beach
just pieces today
leaving the whole ones
for luckier beachcombers
striated gray pink
gastropod cross sections
wind-roughened growth lines
of bivalve halves
radula-drilled holes
in most domed umbos

object permanence is tricky
I take them home to remember
the ocean's profound powers
but plucked from their natural habitat
(sand the color of the soles of your feet)
their effervescent magic dims

when pulled away from who we are
(part of the sea)
we lose our luster too

and so we face a titanic dilemma
when taken inland shells turn to dust
but if left on the shore
do they even exist?

topsail

Drifted away from its smack
A cannonball jellyfish in a sound-side tidal pool
Has neighbors nice enough
Bladderwrack and sargassum
Warpaint shiners and shed crab claws
(A reminder to hold on tight)
Gets poked by a boy freshly emboldened from
    challenging the sea
Armored with trinket-filled pockets and
    fist-sized lophelia
Presently the lighthouse will send the boy to
    bed
After which the moon will lug the cannonball
    out to sea
Being trapped in a microcosm a sunny
    adventure
But our jelly would die without the vast dark
    sea

forever stares back

the sea spits salt and brine
turning stone to sands of time

here where I and infinity meet
the ocean throws itself at my feet

waves break inside my head
but I'm not dead
no I'm not dead

between lakes

I'm not the oracle in the orchard,
but I see sutures in your future.
I went to see her,
turned left on Luster,
past Starland and Grassland,
over Frying Pan Creek,
turned right on Old Mine,
but she wasn't there.
My mom says she's not ripe yet,
like the peaches aren't ripe 'til summer.
You can't have peach cobbler on your birthday,
they aren't ripe in April.
I'm April. It's spring!
You were in the car with me.
You pointed at flowers,
at the trailer with THURSTON in thick script,
looked away from the hawk eating entrails of
  roadkill.
We traveled up gravel,
whistled and winter went running away,
but the orchard oracle wasn't there.
We crashed into a cherry tree.
It shattered into matchsticks.
The windshield splintered into your skin.
I'm not the oracle in the orchard,
but I see sutures in your future.

buried

I kill all my darlings every night,
fling them far, erase to white.
Repeat my lines and the themes I find,
haven't I grown in all of this time?
Blackberries litter the saccharine street,
staining black bruises on rubber-soled feet.
Beating sun eats graffiti,
releases it into porous concrete.
I speed by it, it reads,
in red spraypaint faded brown,
This is not your home, but you are here now.
Well this perplexes me,
it resurrects in me
feelings I'd buried
a decade ago before we married.
Tires screech and spin out in a crash,
fires bleach it all to ash.
A flash in the pan or something true?
You saved my life; I don't owe it to you.

tornado alley

Aware of murders and murmurs of birds
Shrieking away from the supercell storm,
Read the truth in weathered, gray-heathered
  words,
Existence easy; living, an art form.

At midwestern dinners nonconforming,
Downpour of heavenly hail and heartbreak,
This new naked family performing,
Down ground holes like moles, voles, and
  garter snakes.

Farmland cyclone, irate purple vortex,
Tempestuous winds send life down below,
Scorpion and bull clamor past doorsteps,
Full time parenting its own tornado.

Lightning stretches up in gold dendriform,
First gray sky, then thunderstorm, last twisters,
God's science the answer to this blamestorm,
That or the disappointment of sisters.

night vision

I'm up – eyelid-filtered insomnia.
Omniscient visions are what's wrong with us.
Can't differentiate what's happening
From shadowy falsehoods on sleepless
    screens.
Hear the same thunder from roaring airplanes,
Crashing upstairs footfalls, or highway hum.
Feel the same sting from black licking leather,
Scraped skin, or joy-stealing comparison.
Sing the same conversations of closeness,
Confusing love, or exchange of power.
Search the same clock face for hints of
    daylight,
Weak sun streaks, or goodness at this hour.
At first find none, but as minutes creep by,
Words leak through eyelashes instead of light,
Weaving stories of solitude and sight,
Vivid images of both peace and fright –
My purpose for being awake at night.

summer

flow

Equidistant between mountains and sea
The pinnacle of creativity
Lies in life's proclivity
For a flow, high or low, fast or slow
On a boat or on the road
It's deep cuts or it's rainbows
Flowing words, water, bodies, blood
Breath, death, ink, love
Driving on asphalt under mud
Feel the urge to jump the car on the curb
Where leaf piles lay undisturbed
Not for long
Blazing along, blaring a song
About yellow birds and silver wreaths
Shouting our own words as we examine the
    deep
Water in the center of the lake
May those depths heal our cuts and heartache
Ambulance wheels squeal as we drown wide
    awake
A liferaft thrown as we row through decay
Stitches for lady liberty's wounded nation
She can't get an abortion, just objectification
Call her a whore 'cause she likes degradation
Porn is today's sex education
Wound us with words of manipulation
Then just sew us back up
We'll fall down, then stand up
We'll breathe through the flare up
A little shallower than before
Like the scoped-out edges where the lake

meets the shore
Like the fallen leaves mud-stuck to the driver's
    side door
Images that aren't funny anymore
Realizing they never were
But unsure why we were unsure
Dreaming twin unraveling dreams
Sleep ripped at the seams
Split stitches of the car's leather seats
Fall asleep at the wheel
And drift into the lake
Acceptance is not the only fate
Don't wait for tomorrow to become today
Splash awake and drive away
Make ourselves wrench love from hate
Make ourselves pull bliss from pain
From mountains to sea, flow through life's gate

watson

Watching the woods from the window I can't tell
The difference between mountain laurel and
    branching antlers of elk
On our way to hike we got turned around
We stumbled into an artist's fair in a small
    mountain town
We strolled down the walk and stepped into
    stalls
Of artisan wares on the lawn of town hall
We touched bowls of carved burls and an
    antler pendant
That fell from the crown of a white tail
    resplendent
We looked and looked for a mug for your
    mother
But none fit in the palm as well as the other
Which had broken upon the floor where it
    clattered
Had it been covered in velvet it wouldn't have
    shattered
Instead we chose a tulip poplar leaf
And curled it into a cup for tea
It won't replace broken pottery
But green leaves with lobes like antler tines
Remind us of blissful green summer times

summer

I'm not a liar but I've lied
I'm not an addict but can't quit
It happens inside white riptides
Where all our multitudes don't fit
Complaining about womanhood
And anxious over lovers past
You lay me down on cedarwood
With cypress knees along the path
Favorite seasons differ slightly
Last summer was the promised land
Though December moon glows whitely
If spring's a sin, then I'll be damned

war

wrestling with dread existential
my weakness is Achilles' temple
tendencies for well-heeled objects
undiminished exhibitionism complex
healing powers
scalding showers
climbing up blue belltowers
secret lives stay confidential
photographs in golden hours
male gaze upon earning potential
waking up red wallflowers
our separateness inconsequential
downfalls of Trojan horsepower

unapologetic

I stole a bottle
full of pennies
shaped like bottle
nose dolphins
I can't be trusted
all those pennies
now are rusted
hit the throttle
I've fallen
and busted
my cover
disgusted
my mother
dusted
and discovered
myself stealing change
my faulty brakes
are no one's fault
it's one default
or another
as a kid full of salt
I stole an undercover
CD about lovers
explicit lyric stickers
exchanged
for censored content
I'm maladjusted
not deranged
I'm hellbent
but short-changed
well-meant
my brand of strange

I spent
what I earned
what I stole
to soothe the burn
and ease my soul
I'm empathetic
to the discontent
and concerns
of the whole
the magnetic
spinning earth
and its poles
the prophetic
nature of children
with no control
I stole
a ticket
to a flight out west
I'm unapologetic
I'm doing my best

whole foods basket

my new purse
a stolen whole foods basket
a gift
from my father
the basket thief
thanks dad
in the basket
a buried memory
of a college boss
he told me
the uniform was short skirts
he sold me
on private personal training
as an employment benefit
he was the trainer
he came to my house
he told me
to get dressed
in clothes he brought
I tried them on
he cut them
even shorter
with scissors
not even evenly
jagged and ragged
he put me
through a hard workout
in my living room
my dog growled and snarled
so I locked her
apologizing
in the bedroom

where she barked and barked
(I'm sorry Lady)
I quit
the next morning on the phone
I told him
to fuck off
my dad tried
to chase him down
at his business
scare the shit out of him
but he didn't
find him
it's okay
I got away
thanks anyway
dad

youth

When you move to four different states
In childhood
Moving is no longer frightening
No scary bogeymen in new-to-you closets
Moving is just heavy
And daunting
Until a new space is claimed
Not conquered but conjured
But to pack our boxes
And the bags under our eyes
And move away from youth
Is terrifying indeed

lists

I fell asleep in front of the fire
Woke up burning deep inside her
Ash from the inside out the outside in
The taste of charred skin
Burn it off
Burn them gone
Turning on the spit
Over the open flame of the fire pit
That's what I get
They said
Don't put bumper stickers on a Bentley
But if Audrey Kawasaki
Van Gogh or Dali
Offered to paint your car
To make you a star
It would be a far
Cry to say no
We saw a doe
She snorted hello
With curiosity that killed
The cat-faced girls
Tore their limbs and cut their curls
Read their skin to the lifeless world
Their words breathless
Their bodies restless
Their thoughts reckless
Informed and inspired
By the fire
In the words of William Carlos Williams
Gibran and Waheed
I suck them in with burning need
They feed

My morbid curiosity
Help me fulfill the prophecy
Let me run down future streets
The future speaks
To those who dream
In the grocery store or the cold mountain
    stream
Bathe my skin in shower steam
By the light of the fire and the bright
    moonbeams
Fireflies alight on the balance beam
You fell off the stone wall
Your body made hard landfall
I told you
My skin won't break your fall

confusing lovers with lovers

I've been counting in odd numbers lately
it feels good
like stepping on cracks
or driving with tires on either side of the line

last night I sat outside
the moon flirted with me through the leaves
we took a walk
he said
it's well lit here at night; we could pretend it's
   another day
so we did
we stayed awake all night
we smoked in the grass
we thought about
midnight picnics
and swore that next time
we would bring a blanket

hail

Woke to neighbors fighting at the window.
It was hail on the brink of bursting through,
Like the newly formed true version of you,
Crumbling from inside out your past statue.
Cut the wires to those dated buttons,
Like button eyes, pushing them does nothing,
Current circuits buzzing, up and running,
Rewired to become your own mother.
Fear not. Be brave. Keep your eyes on the
    stars.
Wipe off the sleep and become who you are.
Bullets shot do not kill men of kevlar.
It's dusty from emergence, your armor,
So polish it. You are new. You are you.

net

Put a net over my mouth to catch the mean
  things
Tried to stitch my lips but couldn't take the sting
My poems aren't confessions
You squeeze them and compress them
Into brittle cubes and flattened squares
Whispering hard words as you pull my hair
Clanging anger then charged quiet
Even the music has gone silent
Escape to pine silhouettes and hills of daisies
Windows down, wet, sweat, summer hazy
Weaving through woods on dirt roads and
  switchbacks
Hoping that curses and fortunes aren't fact
Lizards skitter over mountain-faced slate
Down memory lane to my namesake lake
With one hand on the wheel or none at all
Driving through paintings of covered bridges in
  fall
A space where the attention is in my control
Attention for pieces, rarely the whole
I contain multitudes and my words do too
Even when they're misconstrued, even when
  they're painted blue
Your bubble floated up and met hail
My train's underwater, yours is a monorail
For every nymph who skipped from the forest:
You words are gorgeous, your soul is glorious
For every poet with red roots and black ink:
You are more complete than you think

temple

The floors of old wooden houses slant
In places of prayer worshippers can't
Lift houses or bowed heads to see the blue sky
(With palms rested on thighs)
Blue the only hue not in your eyes
So I never see blue
(I only look at you)
I see red
I ride past flowers of orange
You replaced another door hinge
In my house with slanted floors
The enchanted forest
The temple in which god bows before us

eyes

take bright eyes for pain as needed
to gray it out or to feed it
feed myself but can't taste the food
a waste of a good mood
shifted into a bad attitude
sifted through sand in search of you
hunted Orion in the sky with Artemis
she shot him down, I did the rest
an arrow right through the heart
right through the eye
right through the soul
doing the right thing takes its toll
cost is high, morale is low
worth every penny – is it though?
cracked coins on the floor
spare change in the drawer
trying to change, but what's it for?
suspicion knocking at the door
you'll win your battles
I'll see you after the war
cards spell out abundance
reading them gets redundant
I know what I need
I know what I've seen
my knowing is growing and fighting in me
I want to lie down
I'm so tired you see
I'm inspired by smoke rings
and waves on the sea
my finger, your red ring
you keep choosing red things
watch, belt, and red dreams

send me to bed dreams
apply pressure to my decompressing
spirit and soul
one small part of the whole
my heart's in control
at the wheel
fall asleep while I feel
summer plans flying
intuition rising
like the sun
you're my one
I love you in spite of me
you're not my keeper
you will never be
only I can feed myself to the sea
to the stars
to the skies
look at me
give me your eyes

seeds

run my fingers through your soft salted hair
they're bloody from biting and slicing your
   pears
it's hard to look away when under your stare

you keep peeling peaches down to their pits
when it's all peeled away what still exists
the seed of a soul on which I subsist

hands

I'm polite.
I don't shine as brightly when time's not
  matched.
Hold me tight
With your left-handed snuffbox so
  scar-patched.
I turn my poems into songs,
Can't help but badly sing along,
As I fall madly into wrong
Worries that I'll grow too attached.

Mollusk holes
In the sand, an impermanent command,
Like the whole
Circle of unhanded wedding bands.
Two well-matched hands at ten and two,
Your pickup truck driving straight through
To wherever home is for you.
I'll visit if you hold both of my hands.

vowels

obsession
with assonance
avoidance until
clairvoyance appears
bending words to my will
interlocking
interlacing
upside down
rearranging
until verse
stamped and carried
away on your heart
matched up
and put down
once again falls apart

reach

Getting lost in the catacombs
I forget that I'm not alone
Green pastures and missed connections
Mountains, streams, and self-reflections
I blaze on
Keep my gaze on
What's ahead
Respectfully revisit the dead
Go left, right, and where I'm led
Successfully get out of my head
Just need a lawn chair to laze on
To make clouds of gray haze on
The porch on the beach
On the sand where we wed
With crashing waves and my ring of red
I escape to the sea to be
Alone or with a piece of me
My own blissful ocean Awakening
Then I'm back in the woods in the trees
Bathed in a fresh sea of green
I go forward and sideways in these caves
Their firelit crypts and passageways
Lead to vistas near and far away
The mind is a funny place
Backyards, mountains, beaches, lakes,
Highways, dry days, and old heartaches
In the catacombs it's not just me
Everywhere is within reach

men

titles are like rocks in my pocket
or the red nosecone of my son's toy rocket
a small reminder of a bigger idea
a tiny token of a torrent
I crack them open with a real hammer
sparks fly like the fourth of July
out rivers of words pour
about men I love or loved before
rivers swelling and shrinking
without even thinking
a whole world written
in one sentence unfinished
men…

about the author

Smyth Rose is a curious creature and a creative soul. She has been writing since childhood and finds herself inspired by relationships, nature, science, art, and kink. Smyth understands the plurality within each of us. She resides on the east coast between mountains and sea. *men* is her publishing debut.

www.ingramcontent.com/pod-product-compliance
Lightning Source LLC
Chambersburg PA
CBHW070545160726
48003CB00005B/1896